Habitat Destruction

by Helen Orme

By Helen Orme

Series consultant: Terry Jennings

ticktock editor: Sophie Furse

ticktock designer: Hayley Terry

Picture research: Lizzie Knowles

With thanks to: Joe Harris, Mark Sachner and Claire Lucas

Copyright © ticktock Entertainment Ltd 2008
First published in Great Britain in 2008 by ticktock Media Ltd,
Unit 2, Orchard Business Centre, North Farm Road,
Tunbridge Wells, Kent, TN2 3XF

ISBN 978 1 84696 736 8 pbk
Printed in China

Picture credits
age fotostock/ Superstock: OFC . A.N.T Photolibrary/ NHPA: 27c. blickwinkel/ Alamy: 18br. Digital Vision/ Photolibrary Group:
25. David R Frazier Photolibrary, Inc./ Alamy: 14-15. Greg Gardner/ iStock: 10t. Glow Images/ Photolibrary Group: 9t.
iStock: 1, Sander Kamp/ iStock: 18cr. Peter Oxford/ Nature Picture Library/ Rex Features: 18tr. Photographers Choice/
Photolibrary Group: 12c. Pixtal/ SuperStock: 28b. Jeffrey L. Rotman/ Corbis: 19t. Shutterstock: 4-5, 5t, 6-7, 7t, 8-9, 10,
11b, 13, 15tl, 15tr, 16-17, 17t, 19, 20t, 22-23, 24t, 26t, 26b 27b, 29, 30, 31, 32. Clint Spencer/ iStock: 20-21. Martin
Strmko/ iStock: 28t. ticktock Media Archive: 13c, OBC. Ivanov Valeriy/ iStock: 2
Every effort has been made to trace the copyright holders, and we apologise in advance for any unintentional omissions.
We would be pleased to insert the appropriate acknowledgements in any subsequent edition of this publication.

CONTENTS

Words that appear **in bold** are explained in the glossary.

AMAZING HABITATS

Just think of all the different places in the world where wild plants and animals live – **rainforests***, deserts, prairies, polar regions, mountains, oceans, even parks and gardens.*

The place where an animal or plant lives is called its habitat. Each animal and plant has adapted to its habitat. Everything it needs to survive is there.

So, if a **habitat** is damaged or destroyed, wildlife can't just move somewhere else. If this happens it can be a disaster, and plants and animals can become **extinct**.

Ring-tailed lemurs live in the forests of Madagascar. To protect these animals we must also protect their habitat.

EARTH'S GROWING POPULATION

Our planet's population is increasing. In 1950 there were two and a half billion people in the world. By 2050 there will be over nine billion people.

This growth means that we need more food, water, and clothes. We also need materials for our homes and roads, such as wood, stone, metals and fuels **mined** from the ground.

In order to supply all of these things, many natural habitats are being destroyed. This means there are fewer places for plants and animals to live.

The growth of modern towns and cities make natural habitats get smaller, or even disappear completely. One day, this town in the desert may have grown to the size of the city below.

LAND FOR CROPS

In order to feed Earth's growing population, more food needs to be produced. However, there is not enough **fertile** soil to do this. So, for hundreds of years, many forests have been cut down and grasslands cleared.

In the last 2,000 years, many natural habitats in Europe and North America have been destroyed to make room for more people and their crops. Now this is also happening in Asia, South America, and Africa, where rainforests and other habitats are disappearing – fast.

We need to find a way to save these wild habitats and also feed everybody.

OIL PALMS

In Indonesia and
Malaysia, ancient
rainforests are
being cut down to
make room for palm
trees. Palm oil from
these trees is used to make
products like soap and margarine.
The rainforests are also home to millions of plants
and animals. However, as their habitat is slowly
destroyed, many of these now face extinction.

*As Earth's population continues to
grow, more farms like this one will
need to be created. That could mean
more habitats are destroyed.*

9

This plane is spraying crops with pesticides.

These combine harvesters can accidentally kill plants and animals while they are harvesting crops.

INTENSIVE FARMING

To feed everyone in the world, farmers don't just need more land to grow things. They need to grow more food on the land they have. This is called **intensive farming***.*

Intensive farming means using more machines to grow more crops. Machines can work much faster, and for much longer than people.

Intensive farming also means using more **pesticides** to get rid of weeds and insects more quickly. These pesticides can harm the habitat, endangering animals that eat poisoned plants and insects.

Intensive farming may also use chemical fertilizers to make crops grow faster. These can pollute nearby water habitats, killing wildlife.

TIMBER FROM THE RAINFOREST

*The increase in human population also means more homes are needed. Most of the trees used for building homes and furniture come from **sustainable** forests.*

This means that once the trees are cut down, more trees are planted to replace them. Wildlife habitats will be damaged, although they will eventually grow back. Then the wildlife that has been driven out will return.

People love mahogany for making beautiful furniture.

Rainforest timber like **mahogany** is valuable because it is strong and attractive. Once these trees are cut down, the land is usually cleared for crops or for grazing cattle. This land will never fully return to being a wildlife habitat unless the trees are replanted.

The golden-headed lion tamarin is endangered because its rainforest habitat is being destroyed.

PROTECTING BRAZIL

In just 10 years, an area of rainforest twice the size of Portugal was destroyed in Brazil. There is good news, however. The government has created new laws to protect the rainforest.

River Jiparaná

This map shows how much forest has been destroyed. Tropical rainforest is shown as bright red. Pale red and brown areas are cleared land. Burned areas appear black.

DAMAGE FROM MINING

Many useful or valuable materials come from the ground. These include metals such as iron, copper, or gold and fuels like oil, gas and coal.

Many of these materials are found in the ground underneath habitats like rainforests or grasslands. They must be mined, or removed from the ground.

Heavy machinery is used to remove rock and soil, and **extract** the metals and fuels. Roads are built to transport the mined materials. It is impossible to mine an area without damaging the habitat. Mining also kills or drives out the plants and animals that live there.

In 2007, a company in Armenia got permission to mine for copper. Some people are worried that animals living nearby like this Syrian Brown bear and short-toed eagle will be endangered.

A copper mine in Utah, USA.

USING TOO MUCH WATER

Everyone uses water at home and school. This water has to come from rivers, lakes, reservoirs or wells.

The problem is that more water is being used by people than is being replaced by rain. Many rivers and lakes are now beginning to dry up.

With less water, wildlife that lives in or by these rivers and lakes will be unable to survive. Fish and freshwater plants will die, and other animals will be forced to leave. Some species of animals and plants could even become extinct.

THE RIVER THAT IS RUNNING OUT

The Rio Grande River forms part of the border between the USA and Mexico. It is one of North America's longest rivers and was once one of the greatest rivers in the world. So much water has been used by people living nearby, however, that it is now drying up.

RAINFORESTS AT RISK

Rainforests are home to the greatest number of plant and animal species on Earth. Many of these are very useful to us. Some plants provide materials for rubber and other products. Some can be used to make medicines.

Rosy periwinkle is an important ingredient of some cancer drugs.

Rainforest plants also help to absorb the **carbon dioxide** in Earth's **atmosphere**. Carbon dioxide is a gas that helps keep the Sun's heat in the atmosphere. If there is too much carbon dioxide in the atmosphere, however, Earth may become too warm.

Rubber is made by cutting into a rubber tree and collecting the sap.

Scientists think this **global warming** has already begun. If we keep destroying rainforests, the effects of global warming on habitats everywhere would be very serious.

Some malaria drugs are made from the bark of the cinchola tree.

OCEANS IN DANGER

The oceans, which cover nearly three-quarters of the world, are another habitat in danger. **Overfishing** takes more fish than can be replaced naturally. Pollution can be a problem too, with oil, litter, chemicals, and sewage dumped into the sea and killing wildlife.

Hotter temperatures around the world may melt ice at the
North and South Poles.

CLIMATE CHANGE AND HABITATS

Climate *change in the form of global warming can be a big cause of habitat destruction. Climate change used to happen slowly, over long periods of time. Recently, however, scientists have noticed the climate changing more quickly.*

These changes include rising temperatures, which may dry out rainforests and swamps. If this happens, millions of plant and animal species that cannot adapt to changes in their habitats may become extinct.

These climate changes began about 100 years ago but have sped up in the last 50 years. Scientists think these changes are caused by things people do today.

PROTECTING THE PLANET

One big cause of habitat destruction is population growth. Another is climate change due to global warming. These two causes are connected.

With more and more people on the planet, their effect on the climate increases. People drive more cars that put carbon dioxide into the atmosphere. There are about 625 million cars in the world today. In 20 years' time, there may be twice as many.

Carbon dioxide causes climate change that can bring on flooding and storms, which threaten nature's habitats. As people clear rainforests and build more buildings, heavy machines increase the levels of carbon dioxide as well as destroying habitats.

If we wish to stop this destruction of Earth's habitats, we must protect the planet from damage caused by both population growth and climate change.

RAINFOREST FACTS

Here are some basic rainforest facts to give you an idea of how important rainforests are to the health of our planet's habitats:

- More than 20% of the **oxygen** people breathe is produced in the Amazon rainforest.

- Rainforests are full of plants that may be useful for food and medicine.

Logging is a major cause of rainforest destruction.

- 2,000 square metres of rainforest are destroyed every second as trees are cut down for their timber. New roads are also built to transport the timber out of the forest.

- Once the rainforest is cut down, the land is used mainly for grazing cattle. The rainforest plants that were once there are not be replaced.

- Scientists believe that every day about 137 different plant or animal species disappear forever.

The dark green areas on this world map show where rainforests are located.

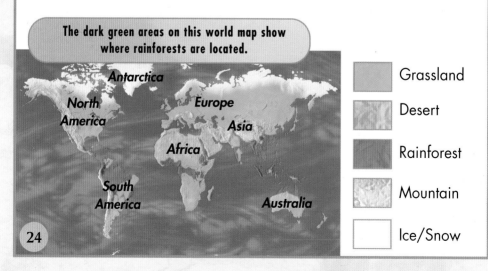

Antarctica

North America

Europe

Asia

Africa

South America

Australia

Grassland

Desert

Rainforest

Mountain

Ice/Snow

FOOD FOR THOUGHT

Here are some things we can do to help reduce the damage caused by using our planet's habitats to provide food:

• Fish are an important part of the habitats they live in – they control plants and algae as well being food themselves. Overfishing can damage the habitats where fish live. Look for fish that are 'line caught' or that come from 'sustainable fisheries'. Line-caught fish are usually caught in low enough numbers that they will not be overfished. Sustainable fisheries also make sure they keep a balance among all members of a habitat.

• Organic food is produced without using chemicals that damage wildlife. It often costs more than non-organic food – but it can be cheaper than buying processed food in packets – and it's better for you!

• Look for food that is labelled 'Fairtrade'. Fairtrade food, such as bananas, coffee or tea, is sold at prices that give a better income to the people who grow them. It also means that the food was grown in a way that does not harm habitats.

ENVIRONMENTALLY FRIENDLY CHOCOLATE

An important ingredient of chocolate bars is cocoa. Cocoa comes from the seeds of the cacao tree, which grows in tropical places.
The story behind chocolate is not as 'sweet' as you might think!

Cocoa is used to make chocolate bars.

• Huge areas of tropical forests have been cleared to make room for cacao trees.

• Cacao trees only live for about 30 years. By then, all the goodness in the soil is used up, so more forest has to be cleared to plant new trees.

Now scientists are finding better ways to grow cacao. Here are two of them:

• Mixed planting. The cacao trees are grown with a mix of other crops, providing a habitat for more birds and animals.

• Looking after the trees. New ways of pruning and caring for the trees mean that they can be more productive and last longer.

These cacao pods can grow up to 35 centimetres long.

KEEPING THE BALANCE

In every habitat, there has to be a balance between the animals and plants that live there. Introducing a new species can upset that balance.

• In 1859, a farmer in Australia released 24 wild rabbits from Europe. Within 10 years, there were over two million of that species in Australia!

• The rabbits have upset the balance of native Australian habitats. They have eaten plants that other species of mammals, birds, and insects depend on for food and shelter. They have contributed to the extinction of other animal species.

Rabbits in Australia have eaten some native plants into extinction.

WHAT CAN BE DONE?

• Countries are now very careful about what animals and plants they allow in. Controlling this can be difficult, however. Insects from other countries can cause huge problems. These could arrive without anyone knowing, on a ship or a plane, or in plants or fruit from abroad.

CORAL REEFS

Coral reefs are one of the world's richest and most beautiful habitats. Coral is made from the skeletons of tiny animals called polyps.

A diver watching fish at a coral reef.

- Coral reefs can be damaged or destroyed by pollution, overfishing, and rough treatment from ships or divers. Reefs may be destroyed when parts of them are taken away for making jewellery. Higher sea temperatures caused by global warming may upset this habitat's balance and also reduce coral populations.

WHAT CAN WE DO?

- The most important thing is to protect the reefs we still have. One way is to teach people how to handle coral in a way that won't damage or destroy it.

Artificial reef balls off the coast of the Caribbean island of Curaçao.

- Another thing we can do is build artificial reefs. This is a hard surface for barnacles, corals and other sealife to grow on. All sorts of things have been used for artificial reefs – concrete blocks, rubble from buildings, even sunken ships and oil rigs!

HOLIDAYS AND TRAVEL

People love to travel to see wildlife in different parts of the world. This can, however, cause damage to the environment:

• Gases produced by aeroplanes can increase global warming, and new airports can cover huge areas of the country with buildings and runways. These take up a lot of space, therefore destroying more habitats and disturbing plants and animals. Just travelling around can disturb the wildlife.

Air travel is more harmful to the environment than travelling by car or train.

• Tourists need hotels, which need lots of space, power and water.

• This doesn't mean people should stop travelling, though. Tourists bring money into less wealthy countries, and tourism creates jobs. Visitors may also provide money to help wildlife projects.

• No one wants to visit places where the wildlife has disappeared. So we need to make sure we protect the habitats in our home country and in the countries we visit as well.

Money from these tourists will help to save endangered habitats.

WHAT YOU CAN DO

• Do you have a wildlife area at your school? Even schools in cities may be able to find room to display plants, shells and other objects collected from local habitats.

• Visit and support nature reserves in the area where you live. You could even be a volunteer and help run them.

• Find out where your food comes from. Fish from sustainable sources and organic or Fairtrade food help protect against habitat destruction.

• Join an organization like the World Wildlife Fund that supports protecting endangered habitats and the animals that live in them, like this baby orang-utan.

Visit these websites for more information and to find out how you can help save habitats.

World Wildlife Fund: www.wwf.org

Fish4Ever campaign: www.fish4ever.org

BBC: www.bbc.co.uk/nature/animals/conservation

GLOSSARY

adapted Changed or suited to fit into a particular situation or habitat.

atmosphere The air, and gases that surround our planet.

carbon dioxide A gas given off when things decay or are burnt.

climate Patterns of weather over a long period of time.

extinct A species of animal or plant that has disappeared forever.

extract To remove.

fertile Rich in substances that help plants grow; capable of growing in great numbers or quantity.

global warming The warming of the planet's air and oceans as a result of a build-up of greenhouse gases in the atmosphere.

habitat The place that suits a particular animal or plant in the wild.

intensive farming Using money, equipment, and chemicals to get more crops and other food products out of less land.

mahogany A heavy, strong, wood, often used to make furniture.

mined Removed from deep inside the Earth.

overfishing Taking more fish from a body of water than can be replaced naturally.

oxygen A gas in the Earth's atmosphere. Humans and most animals need oxygen to breathe.

pesticides Chemicals that kill animals or plants that damage crops.

pollute To release harmful substances into the environment.

rainforest Huge forests of tall trees. Rainforests are normally warm and have lots of rain.

sustainable Something that can be used into the future without using up resources, or made in a way that will last forever.

INDEX